Panorama-Books: POMPEII

With thirty color plates

STANLEY A. JASHEMSKI

POMPEII

and the Region destroyed by Vesuvius in A. D. 79

Text and Notes by

WILHELMINA F. JASHEMSKI

University of Maryland

MUNICH

ANDERMANN OHG PUBLISHERS

Wrapper and cover designed by Gerhard M. Hotop

1971

© 1965 by Wilhelm Andermann Verlag, Munich
Printed in Germany. 165

One August afternoon, almost 1900 years ago, a seventeen year old boy named Pliny looked across the Bay of Naples and saw a cloud of unusual size and appearance. Young Pliny was visiting his uncle, the famous elder Pliny, commander of the Roman fleet stationed at Misenum across the Bay from Naples. To Pliny the Elder, a well known natural scientist, the strange cloud, shaped like an umbrella pine, sometimes white, sometimes dark and spotted, appeared to be a remarkable phenomenon worth observing at closer range. As he was preparing to depart a plea for help came from friends living near the base of Vesuvius, for the destructive cloud was issuing from that volcano. Hastening across the Bay and finding it impossible to land because of the turbulence of the sea, he turned his course toward Stabiae. There he lost his life in attempting to rescue friends. Years later the Roman historian Tacitus wrote to Pliny the Younger asking for details regarding his uncle's death. Fortunately the two letters written in reply have been preserved giving us a vivid eye-witness report of the eruption in A. D. 79.

For two days Vesuvius spewed forth a mixture of ashes and pumice stone, followed by volcanic dust accompanied by successive earthquake shocks. Twisting and vibrating streaks of flame broke through the dark and dreadful cloud above Vesuvius and young Pliny believed that the whole world was perishing with him. But Misenum was more fortunate than the regions across the Bay nearer to Vesuvius.

When the eruption ceased on the second day, Pompeii was covered to a depth of from nineteen to twenty-three feet. The villas in the vicinity of Stabiae, although farther from Vesuvius, suffered a similar fate. At Herculaneum, a small town on the western slope of Vesuvius, the volcanic debris was mixed with great volumes of rain that made it into a torrent of mud which penetrated into every crevice of the ancient town, and covered it to a depth of from thirty to sixty feet.

Most of the inhabitants fled, but in the darkness many were trampled to death on the roads leading outside the cities, or were overcome by the fumes. Of course those who stayed behind perished.

First Excavation and Rediscovery

As soon as the ashes settled the survivors went back to Pompeii to rescue valuables. Roofs of houses that had not caved in furnished guideposts for these first "excavators" who dug down into the buried city at recognizable places, and from there tunneled from room to room to remove valuables, such as furniture, jewelery, money, important documents and records – even the marble facings of the buildings about the Forum.

The Roman Emperor Titus sent a senatorial commission to Campania to study the situation and make plans to rebuild the buried cities, but apparently nothing was done. During the Middle Ages even the name of Pompeii was forgotten.

The ruins were first discovered in the sixteenth century by the architect Domenico Fontano who tunneled under Pompeii to build a water channel (still in use) to bring water from the Sarno River to Torre Annunziata. Two inscriptions and remains of buildings found at the few points where the tunnel reached the surface created little interest. Excavations did not begin at Pompeii until 1748; it was only in 1763 that an inscription was found which identified the site as Pompeii. Excavations have continued with intermittent interruptions until today about two-thirds of the ancient city have been excavated. Earlier digging was haphazard; excavators were primarily treasure seekers, hunting for imposing buildings and important museum objects. Pictures were cut from walls, statues and fine articles were collected; these were then carted off to the Museum in Naples without even recording the location of their origin. A site that yielded nothing of obvious value was quickly abandoned and a more promising one sought.

Excavations began earlier at Herculaneum (1709) but work progressed very slowly. Through the centuries the fill has hardened into a rocklike substance that is exceedingly difficult to remove. The work of excavation is further complicated by the fact that the modern town of Resina is built on top of ancient Herculaneum. The buildings that must be removed are so old, however, that slum clearance and archaeology go hand in hand. Scarcely seven city blocks have been excavated thus far.

At Stabiae in addition to the haphazard excavating between 1749 and 1782 three villas have been carefully excavated since 1950.

FERTILE CAMPANIA

Pompeii, Herculaneum, and Stabiae were situated in the fertile volcanic plain of Campania, famous since antiquity for its incomparable beauty, the fertility of its soil – it yielded as many as four crops a year – and the popularity and fragrance of its flowers. The ancient geographer Strabo called it "the most blest of all plains," and the poet Propertius described it as "fat" Campania. Pliny the Elder rhapsodized over its "blissful and heavenly loveliness" and spoke of its famed roses. Florus praised the flowers of Campania, and called it "the fairest of all regions, not only in Italy, but in the whole world."

Vesuvius which rises in stark majesty in the midst of the Campanian plain continually enriches the land. The last eruption (in March 1944) sprinkled volcanic ash to a depth of almost twelve inches over the surrounding countryside. The rich soil continues to yield three or more crops a year as it did in antiquity.

Since their first discovery, the buried cities of Campania have fired the imagination of both the layman and the scholar. Bulwer Lytton's *Last Days of Pompeii* has implanted in many a young reader the desire to go to Pompeii and visit the House of Glaucus and walk along the streets through which the blind girl Nydia led the lovers Glaucus and Ione to safety when the eruption of Vesuvius had darkened the city.

The magic of the ancient city casts its spell upon all who tarry there. Yet Pompeii was not an important city in antiquity, nor did it play a significant role in the pages of history. It is its golden mediocrity that is its charm. It is typical of so many towns in the Roman Empire, but because of its sudden and tragic destruction by Vesuvius it is a unique archaeological site. Only at Pompeii can the visitor walk up and down miles of streets and visit the homes, temples, and places of business of thousands of former inhabitants. For this reason Pompeii is still an unexhausted source of information for those who would know more about how people lived, worked, worshiped, and played in the Roman Empire. By ancient standards Pompeii was not a small town; the city walls enclosed 161 acres. Herculaneum was a much smaller town.

Pompeii and Herculaneum had not always been Roman towns. It was not until 89 B. C. that they were besieged by the Roman general Sulla, and it is possible that Herculaneum as well as Pompeii was made a Roman colony in 80 B. C. The origins of both towns are lost in antiquity, but legend recounts that they were both founded by the hero Hercules on his return from Spain. We do know, however, that both cities were many centuries old when they were conquered by the Romans. The earliest building at Pompeii, the remains of a Doric temple, believed to be built in honor of Hercules, goes back to the sixth century B. C., but a settlement at Pompeii is probably at least two centuries older.

As the visitor enters Pompeii through the Porta Marina (Gate to the Sea) and climbs the steep road leading to the Forum, he passes on the right the ruined temple of Venus Pompeiana, the tutelary deity of the city. On the left is the temple of Apollo. (No fewer than ten temples have been discovered thus far at Pompeii.)

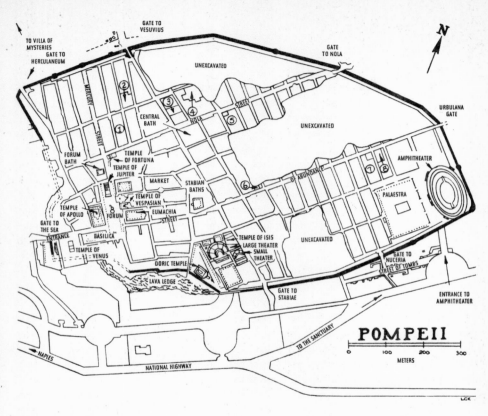

1. House of The Faun
2. House of the Vettii
3. House of L. Caecilius Jucundus
4. House of L. Albucius Celsus
5. House of T. Claudius Verus
6. Shop of Verecundus
7. House of M. Loreius Tiburtinus
8. House of Venus Marina

After entering Pompeii the visitor should stop and linger in the Forum. This great rectangular piazza was the center of the religious, economic, and political life of the city, and was surrounded with temples, civic buildings, markets and exchanges. No other Italian or Roman town could boast a Forum with such a grandiose setting. Towering behind the magnificent temple on the north end of the Forum dedicated to the Capitoline triad, Jupiter, Juno, and Minerva, was the menacing bulk of Vesuvius. Behind the municipal buildings on the south end of the Forum, the Lattari Mountains furnished an impressive backdrop. On the east side were two small temples; the one dedicated to the worship of the emperor, the other thought to have been built to the City Lares in expiation, after the earthquake of A. D. 62. The ruined state of the buildings in the Forum, even today, impresses upon the visitor the magnitude of the calamity which destroyed so much of Pompeii and the surrounding area. This earthquake was so severe that a flock of 600 sheep was reported killed, and many people were said to have lost their reason. Scarcely a building in Pompeii escaped damage. The inhabitants had not completed the rebuilding of their city, when seventeen years later the final catastrophe overtook them. Most of the Forum was still unrestored; not even the Capitoline temple had been rebuilt. Homes were given first priority.

Two buildings, important in the economic life of the city were located on the east side of the Forum. In the Macellum, the large provision market, townsmen could purchase everything for a dinner party from fish to garlands of flowers. Live sheep were also available. The headquarters of the perfume manufacturers and sellers was located in two of the second story shops on the front of the Macellum. The imposing edifice built by the priestess Eumachia as the headquarters of the woolen industry furnishes eloquent testimony of the importance of wool in the Pompeian economy; the many fulleries that have been excavated in the city enable the visitor to see the actual establishments in which the wool was processed.

Even today sheep are not an unusual sight at Pompeii. Early in the morning one may meet on the mainstreet of the modern city a shepherd leading his flocks to pasture, with two black goats bringing up the rear. Or on returning home from the excavations in the evening, I have heard the tinkle of sheep bells and looked up to see sheep grazing near the walls of the amphitheater.

The meticulously sculptured marble border around the entrance of the wool hall (known as the Eumachia), is the only marble decoration in the Forum that has escaped the ancient salvagers. Amid a design of leaves and flowers, are many birds and insects that delight the person who lingers to look at them. Further inspection reveals a bird swallowing a grasshopper, an owl teasing a mouse, even the ubiquitous lizard which today inhabits the ruins.

Of special significance in a commercial city was the *mensa ponderaria*, the table containing the official liquid and dry measures, found on the west side of the Forum. A close examination shows that the original cavities in the table were enlarged, and the old names of the measures erased, when the Pompeian measures were brought into conformity with the Roman standard. An inscription on the edge of the table names the magistrates who "in accordance with a decree of the city council caused the measures to be made equal" to the Roman measures.

The most imposing building facing the Forum was the Basilica; its identification is certain for the word *basilica* was scratched by idlers on its walls. It served as the meeting place of the courts, as a market, and as the financial center of the city. For this reason it has been likened to the Stock Exchange of a modern city. With its nave and two side aisles, it is similar in floor plan to the later Christian basilicas. This makes the Basilica the most architecturally significant building in the city, and of considerable importance in studying the origin and development of the Christian basilica. Badly destroyed by the earthquake of A. D. 62, it had not yet been restored in A. D. 79. The sturdiness of the columns is impressive; although only stumps have survived, their size suggests that they must have supported a roof over the nave.

The Forum was the heart of the city. Here came country folk with the produce of their farms; merchants displayed finished articles made in Pompeii, as well as in more distant places. A series of sketchy paintings found on the walls of an ancient house on the Via dell'Abbondanza (Street of Abundance) preserves for us a vivid picture of life

11

in the Forum, and shows merchants of every kind selling their wares: the shoemaker, the breadman, the fruit and vegetable woman, the soup seller, the cloth merchant, and the seller of pots and pans. We see men consulting notices on a public bulletin board, a seated scribe waiting for business, children playing hide and seek, and the ever present beggar. Citizens discuss the latest civic question, or the newest gossip. Garlands hanging between the columns of the portico, which surrounds the Forum on three sides, add a festive note. This colonnade furnished welcome shelter from the hot Italian sun, and likewise during inclement weather.

The Forum was also the scene of colorful religious festivals. Before the amphitheater was built, gladiatorial combats were held in the Forum; the choice seats were no doubt in the upper story of the colonnade. We know that musical entertainments, bullfights, and other spectacles were held in the Forum. It was here that the processions that were such an important part of life in an ancient city, were formed.

If the broken stones of the Forum could only talk, what stories they might recount of the stirring political scenes that had taken place there: the exchange of heated arguments before the city decided to join the revolt against the Romans in 90 B. C., the tense occasion when Pompeii was proclaimed a Roman colony after the war, the feverish activity on behalf of favorite candidates each year at election time.

INNS AND RESTAURANTS

Pompeii was a bustling commercial city that enjoyed a large export as well as an import trade. The harbor of Pompeii, at the mouth of the Sarnus River, served as a port for the inland towns of Nuceria and Nola. A picture found on a recently excavated household shrine portrays the ancient boat traffic on the Sarnus and shows porters carrying products to load on boats that ply the river. The river god, Sarnus, was worshiped in many households and played an important role in the life of Pompeii. Preliminary excavations at the port of Pompeii have brought to light evidence

12

of the warehouses and remains of wine and oil amphorae. Other indications of the exports and imports that passed through the port of Pompeii might be mentioned: a jar that had contained fish sauce made at Pompeii, found at Rome; a receipted bill for a linen auction, probably for an Egyptian merchant, found in the home of L. Caecilius Jucundus, the auctioneer at Pompeii; wine amphorae from the Greek islands, Spain, Crete, and Sicily found at Pompeii; pottery from Gaul and lamps from north Italy, not yet unpacked at the time of the eruption.

The merchants and tradesmen who came from great distances as well as from the surrounding countryside could find food and lodging in the many restaurants and inns located throughout the city. Many inns were conveniently located near the city gates; in such places there was frequently room for the traveler as well as for his tired donkey. Other travelers might prefer accommodations near the Forum where they were transacting their business. The largest hotel found thus far had rooms for fifty guests and is located on a winding street a short walk from the Forum. There is evidence that the Christians used this hotel as a meeting place.

Quick lunch counters or bars were conveniently located on almost every block. Some had dark and smoky rooms where guests might be served at tables. But in the ancient city, just as today, the Pompeians as well as visitors to the city enjoyed eating outdoors. Many inns and restaurants had gardens, in which the traveler might accept the invitation of the hostess who, in the words of the ancient poet, bade him "come and rest your weary self beneath the shady vine and bind your head with a chaplet of roses." In such a garden restaurant, guests might be offered "wreaths of violets and crocus blossoms, and yellow garlands mixed with crimson roses, and lilies." Beautiful garlands were abundant in ancient Pompeii, for this city was the center of a large flower industry. Guests might be entertained by dancing girls, accompanied by castanets and pipes. We know the names of a number of the girls who worked in Pompeian inns and restaurants: there is Hedone, the Greek barmaid, famous for her sign which offered a drink for one *as,* a better drink for two, Falerian for four. The girls who worked in the restaurant of Asellina are known from the notices which they put up on the outside of the restaurant recommending candidates in the municipal elections;

there is the Greek girl Aegle, the Hebrew maid Maria, and Smyrna, whose name records her native city. Traders coming to Pompeii from distant countries found it not at all difficult to find a restaurant where their native tongue was spoken. Traders from the East, from Gaul, Africa, and Egypt, and perhaps even from far away India found their way to Pompeii.

TEMPLES AND SHOPS

One of the most popular temples in town was the temple of the Egyptian goddess Isis. The popularity of this cult is attested by the fact that her temple was one of the first to be rebuilt after the earthquake of A. D. 62. An inscription over the entrance to the courtyard of the temple of Isis says: "After the earthquake Numerius Popidius Celsinus, son of Numerius, at his own expense rebuilt the temple of Isis from the ground up. In recognition of his generosity the members of the city council admitted him to their council without cost, even though he was only six years old."

Around the corner from the temple of Isis was the modest temple of Zeus Meilichius, a Greek divinity whose worship was probably introduced from Sicily. The large statues of Jupiter and Juno, and the bust of Minerva found in this temple, indicate that it housed the worship of the Capitoline triad after the earthquake of 62, until the great temple in the Forum could be repaired.

The visitor who walks up and down the streets of the newly excavated parts of the city is transplanted back to A. D. 79. Dishes and a change box can be seen still standing on the counter. Accounts showing what customers owed are scratched on the walls. Bread is found in bakery ovens. The great lava millstones for which Pompeii was famous stand in the many bakeries scattered throughout the city. In the peristyles of many a fine house large vats and dye furnaces had been installed, in which soiled clothes were cleaned and newly woven cloth was prepared for use and dyed. The resident of a modern city who has seen fine old homes made over into rooming houses and places of business, immediately recognizes a similar change taking place at Pompeii. As the old families fled to the suburbs, their city homes were frequently taken over by wealthy freedmen who converted these houses all or in part to commercial use.

An impressive shop sign on the Via dell 'Abbondanza shows Venus Pompeiana, the patron deity of the city, being drawn in hieratic splendor by four elephants. Below is an informative painting which pictures the various steps in the making of woolen cloth. On the right the owner holds up a piece of finished cloth. His name Verecundus is painted in small black letters under his picture. On the opposite side of the door is a painting of the god Mercury with a money bag in his hands. This is the street of merchants and Mercury was their special god. Nearby is the shop of Verus, the copper-smith who was also a land surveyor; his surveying instruments were found in his shop. In the same block Junianus sold tools, as well as harnesses and bridles to the farmers. Felix, the fruit dealer, had his shop on this street, as did Zosimus, whose mutilated shop sign announced that he sold *vasa faecaria*, that is, containers for the fish sauces that were so popular at Pompeii. Fragments of almost every size and shape of terra cotta containers have been found in his shop. On the wall of his shop was a list of the Market Days in the neighboring towns: Saturday was Market Day at Pompeii, Sunday at Nuceria, Monday at Atella, Tuesday at Nola, Wednesday at Cumae, Thursday at Puteoli, Friday at Capua and at Rome!

THE BATHS AT POMPEII

It is difficult for us today to realize the importance of the public baths in the life of the ancient Romans. Not only did they provide elaborate facilities for bathing, complete with dressing rooms, furnace-heated hot baths, and cold baths; they were also places where one could meet friends for pleasant conversation, play games, swim in an outdoor pool, and enjoy refreshments. The well preserved Stabian and Forum Baths furnish our best examples at Pompeii. Both had complete baths for men and for women.

The Roman writer Seneca who lived near a bath describes them vividly: "Sounds are heard on all sides. Just imagine for yourselves every conceivable kind of noise that can offend the ear. The men of more sturdy muscle go through their exercises, and swing their hands heavily weighted with lead. I hear their groans when they strain themselves, or the whistling of labored breath when they breathe out after having held in. If one is rather lazy, and merely has himself rubbed with unguents, I hear the blows of the hand slapping his shoulders, the sound varying according as the massagist strikes with flat or hollow palm. If a ball player begins to play and to count his throws, it's all up for the time being. Meanwhile there is a sudden brawl, or a thief is caught, or there is some one in the bath who loves to hear the sound of his own voice; and the bathers plunge into the swimming pool with loud splashing. These noises, however, are not without some semblance of excuse; but the hair plucker from time to time raises his thin, shrill voice in order to attract attention, and is only still himself when he is forcing cries of pain from some one else, from whose armpits he plucks the hairs. And above the din you hear the shouts of those who are selling cakes, sausages, and sweetmeats, besides all the hawkers of stuff from the cookshops, each with a different and characteristic cry."

HOUSES AND GARDENS

But it is the houses of Pompeii that provide us with the most wonderful documents that the ancient world has left us; the hundreds of houses that have been excavated offer valuable evidence regarding the life and humanity of the ancient world. The ancient Pompeians become real people to the informed traveler who visits their homes. Household shrines tell us the gods the owner worshiped, shops attached to his home reveal his business interests. Election notices painted on the outside of his house record his participation in politics and the candidates he endorsed. The furniture and statues in his home, and the paintings on his walls tell something of his taste.

Only at Pompeii can we trace the evolution of domestic architecture from the Italic dwellings of the fourth and third centuries B. C. to the Roman house of the first

Blick auf Pompeji von einem Turm der Stadtmauer
View of Pompeii from a Tower of the City Wall
Pompéi vue d'une tour des murailles

Blick auf Misenum vom Avernersee
View of Misenum from Lake Avernus
Misène vu du Lac Averne

Steilhang des Lavastroms, auf dem Pompeji gebaut war
Volcanic Ledge on which Pompeii was Built
La coulée de lave sur laquelle Pompéi est construite

Venus Marina
La Vénus Marine

tar mit Opferszene
crifice Scene on Altar
ène de sacrifice sur un autel

Wahlaufruf
Electoral Notice
Inscription électorale

Trittsteine an einer Straßenkreuzung
Stepping Stones at Street Intersection
Dalles de traversée aux angles des rues

Merkur
Mercury
Mercure

Haus des Faun
House of the Faun
La maison du Faune

Bacchus,
der Gott des Weines
Bacchus, God of Wine
Bacchus, dieu du vin

Weinpresse
in der Mysterienvilla

Wine-Press
in the Villa of the Mysteries

Pressoir à raisin,
dans la Villa de Mystères

<

Bacchantinnen
Worshipers of Bacchus
Adorateurs de Bacchus

Gartenbild im Haus der Venus Marina
Garden Painting in the House of Venus Marina
Jardin peint sur un mur de la Maison de la Vénus Marine

*Garten
des M. Lorejus Tiburtinus*
*The Garden
of M. Loreius Tiburtinus*
*Le jardin
de M. Loreius Tiburtinus*

Brunnenfigur
Fountain Statue
Statue de fontaine

Straße im alten Pompeji
Street Scene in Ancient Pompeii
Une rue de l'ancienne Pompéi

Straße im neuen Pompeji
Street Scene in Modern Pompeii
Une rue de la Pompéï moderne

Blick vom Amphitheater auf das moderne Pompeji
Modern Pompeii from the Amphitheater
La Pompéï moderne vue de l'amphithéâtre

Pompejaner lassen die
Passanten Revue passieren
Modern Pompeians Greet
Passers-by
Les «pompéïens» actuels

Das Lattari-Gebirge von der Palästra aus
View toward the Lattari Mountains from the Palaestra
Les Monts Lattari vus de la Palestre

Atrium im Haus des Telephos
in Herculaneum

Atrium of the House
of Telephus at Herculaneum

L'atrium de la Maison
de Télèphe à Herculanum

Ausgrabungen in Herculaneum
unter dem heutigen Resina
Excavating Ancient
Herculaneum from under
Modern Resina
Les fouilles d'Herculanum
(sous l'actuelle Resina)

Fruchtbares Kampanien
Fertile Campania
La Campanie fertile

Staudamm am Sarno
Dam on the Sarno River
Barrage sur la rivière Sarno

Flora
Flore

Blühender Oleander in einem antiken Garten
Oleander Blooming in Ancient Garden
Les lauriers roses

Die Küste bei Stabiae
The Shore at Stabiae
Le rivage à Stabiae

century of the Christian era. The homes of the earliest inhabitants are still unknown to us; all traces are buried under subsequent constructions. But the most impressive residences at Pompeii do not date from the Roman city; they were built by the Samnite inhabitants during the third and second centuries B. C.

One of the best known of the aristocratic Samnite homes is the House of the Faun built in the second century B. C.; it occupies an entire city block and is more imposing than any known palace of contemporary Hellenistic kings. The huge mosaic of Alexander the Great and the Persian King, Darius, at the battle of Issus, now one of the treasures of the Museo Nazionale in Naples, once decorated the floor of the exedra, a handsome reception room which had a view of both peristyle gardens. Beautiful pictures in mosaic are the characteristic decoration of the Samnite houses; wall paintings are not found until the Roman period.

The house of L. Albucius Celsus, another elegant house dating from the Samnite period, is much better preserved and gives the visitor a good idea of the comforts of the atrium-peristyle house. It is known as the House of the Silver Wedding because the King and Queen of Italy came to Pompeii in 1893 to celebrate their silver wedding and part of this house was excavated in their presence. I shall never forget the first time that I visited this house. It was a very hot day, one of the hottest that I have ever known at Pompeii. When we opened the front door and walked into the huge tetrastyle atrium it was very impressive and very cool. Diffused light from the compluvium was reflected on the dark walls of the atrium. It was not difficult to imagine how delightful it must have been when the large impluvium was filled with water and the fountain at the edge made music as it splashed. From the atrium we looked through the high-ceilinged tablinum, into the peristyle garden beyond, once again planted with flowers and shrubs. It was easy to appreciate the sentiment scribbled on the wall by an ancient Pompeian, "How inviting is your house, O Albucius."

The pipes, with stop-cocks in place, attached to the columns in the peristyle, are a reminder that this house was built long before the Romans came to Pompeii, for it was only after the conquerors had built the aqueduct and brought plentiful water into the city that the luxury of fountains could be enjoyed. When it was no longer necessary to use the impluvium in the atrium to collect rain-water for storage in the cistern below, a fountain could be built in the atrium, potted plants set about the fountain, and the atrium transformed into a secondary garden.

One of the most interesting rooms in the house is the beautiful golden yellow room, decorated with painted garlands, which opens off the south side of the peristyle. Long after the house had been excavated, the famous Pompeian epigrapher, Professor Matteo Della Corte, examined the walls of this room and found the scribblings or graffiti written by the children who had studied there. One had written, "If Cicero isn't pleasing to you, you will be whipped" – perhaps echoing the threats of the teacher, whose name was written nearby, accompanied by derogatory appellations scratched in large letters. Quotes from the Latin poet Virgil, as well as the lines of a popular love song were also found on the wall. A graffito found on the Basilica gives the complete song. One of the occupants of the house, quite possibly a daughter of the family, was a girl named Spendusa. On the wall across the street we read, "Marcus loves Spendusa." Perhaps the love-sick girl scribbled the love song on the school-room wall when she should have been studying her Cicero lesson!

From the east side of the peristyle a door led to another huge garden surrounded by a peristyle. There was a large masonry triclinium in the garden where meals could be enjoyed outdoors; when the table was not in use it served as a fountain! The home of Albucius Celsus also included a large private bath, complete with dressing room, hot bath, tepidarium and cold bath. The cold bath was an outdoor swimming pool, located in a delightful garden.

The best known house of the Roman period is the House of the Vettii, which is representative of the comfortable homes of the wealthy merchant class. The rich paintings on the walls of this house are in a remarkable state of preservation, and the peristyle garden with its many statues and fountains left in situ, is again planted with the flowers that bloomed in the ancient garden. Today the fountains of this garden play again in the summer sun, fed by water flowing through the ancient pipes.

These large homes of the wealthy are well known, but scattered throughout the city are many modest homes too small to boast a single peristyle, or even a single tree. Tourists seldom see these homes and scholars have neglected them. But today when we are as much interested in the lives of the many as in the luxuries of the few, these small houses at Pompeii tell us much. There are many little houses in Pompeii, and each one has its unique character. One of the most attractive is on a narrow street just off the busy Via dell'Abbondanza. The garden at the back of the house is visible from the entrance. There is a splashing fountain, from which birds are drinking and behind a low fence are trees and flowering shrubs. Closer inspection reveals, however, that this is not a spacious garden, but a picture of a garden painted on the rear wall. The actual garden, in front of the painted one, is very small and L-shaped – less than a foot and one half wide, and only seven and a half feet long. The plantings in this strip of earth grew in front of the painted garden. It is possible that herbs were included, for they were much used by the Romans. The kitchen is adjacent to the garden. The bones of a donkey were found in the garden at the time of excavation. Frightened when the volcanic ash began to fall, the animal may have fled blindly through the streets until it ran by error into this house and was trapped. On each side of the entrance of this house is a low masonry bench. It was here that clients, formally clad in white togas, sat early in the morning while waiting their turn to make their formal call on their patron, the master of the house. One client scratched his name on the wall above the bench on which he was waiting. The graffito, no longer extant, read: "Symphorus was here on April 2nd." Apparently even the owner of a modest home could boast of several clients whose attendance increased his prestige in the city. After a patron had greeted his clients, he then hastened to call on his own patron. The streets of Pompeii must have swarmed at daybreak with clients making their calls.

The desire for a few flowers and a bit of green appears to have been a basic part of the Roman character. It was the same instinct that made a shopkeeper who lived in rooms above his shop grow a few vines on his balcony, to provide an arbor of shade. In assessing the Roman character, it is well to remember the inhabitants of the small houses in Pompeii, who loved beauty and insisted upon it, even if in their crowded homes they could have only a miniature garden or a potted plant.

ELECTION NOTICES AT POMPEII

Most conspicuous on the streets of Pompeii are the numerous election notices written by professional sign painters on the facades of homes and shops. It is somewhat surprising to the visitor to find the fronts of aristocratic mansions covered with such notices! Pompeii must have been an exciting place at election time. The Roman orator Cicero, who owned a villa at Pompeii, is said to have remarked that it was more difficult to get elected to the city council at Pompeii than to the Senate at Rome. The eminent Pompeian archaeologist and epigrapher, Matteo Della Corte, by studying the election notices at Pompeii was able to identify the homes and places of business of many prominent as well as humble Pompeians. Friends and neighbors enthusiastically supported their candidates. People engaged in the same occupation frequently backed a candidate; the bakers, the barbers, the innkeepers, the dealers in perfume, even the ball players and the chess players had their candidate. Most of the notices followed a general formula, but at times original touches were added. One candidate was recommended because "he will be the watchdog of the treasury." Others were referred to as "upright young men." Even women took part in municipal elections. Taedia Secunda worked hard to have her grandson elected. Another interesting notice informs us that "His little sweetheart is working for the election of Claudius as duovir." Vatia was recommended by "the sneak thieves," "the whole company of late drinkers," and "all the people who are asleep"! One wonders if these signs might not have been put up by the opposition.

HERCULANEUM

The little town of Herculaneum, located only four miles from Vesuvius is much better preserved than Pompeii, but in many respects it is quite different. There are no election notices at Herculaneum, so we shall never know the inhabitants by name as we do in Pompeii. But the many articles that have been found in Herculaneum give us intimate glimpses into the lives of the people who lived there. Both the depth and nature of the fill made it impossible for survivors to rescue their belongings as they did at Pompeii. Wood, cloth, and food – even eggs in a kitchen cupboard, to say nothing of a complete library of Epicurean writings on papyrus, are all perfectly preserved. Perhaps most remarkable is the way in which mud oozing into every crevice of the wood, has preserved wooden beams, stairs, and furniture. A wooden clothes press standing in a fuller's shop, a baby cradle in a bedroom, a beautiful wooden sofa in a gracious room overlooking a garden, give Herculaneum the atmosphere of a living town. One household had an interesting wooden cupboard about five feet high, the top part designed as a classic temple, with two beautifully carved and fluted columns holding up a porch. When the doors of the tiny temple were opened the statuettes of the household gods were found inside. In the cupboard below the mistress of the house had kept her possessions. Another wooden cupboard was found on the second floor in a large house nearby, which had been subdivided into apartments for poorer people. This cupboard contained no statuettes of gods, but in the stucco above it there was a large impression in the shape of the cross. Some scholars believe that converts to the new religion then spreading into Italy, may have lived in this room, and that the low cupboard with a step in front may be a Christian altar. It should not be surprising to find Christians at Herculaneum. Twenty years before Vesuvius erupted the Christians living nearby welcomed the apostle Paul when he landed at Puteoli, near Naples, and persuaded him to tarry with them seven days before continuing his journey to Rome.

Recent excavations at Herculaneum have discovered the Forum, which as at Pompeii was closed to wheel traffic. Near one of the entrances a large sign was found painted on a pillar, which threatened corporal punishment as well as fines to anyone who got the place dirty. The best preserved building found in the Forum area is the shrine of the Augustales, a building devoted to the cult of the Emperor. An inscription on the wall commemorates the banquet given by the college of priests or Augustales when the hall was formally consecrated. A second Bath and a great Palaestra with a huge swimming pool in the center in the form of a cross have also been uncovered in the new excavations.

But at Herculaneum, as at Pompeii, it is the homes that are the most important. Herculaneum was not a large town; the population was probably less than 5000 inhabitants. On the south edge of the town were the aristocratic homes, with impressive terraces and verandas from which their owners could enjoy the view over the Bay of Naples. But in the town there were also the many homes of the humble craftsmen and fishermen who made up a large part of the population. Although one gets the impression that life was quieter in this little town than in nearby Pompeii, even limited excavations show that the inhabitants of Herculaneum were experimenting with new ideas in architecture, and building houses that could be shared by various families. Not infrequently the atrium was abandoned for a courtyard which furnished light and air. For this reason the houses at Herculaneum form an important chapter in the history of domestic architecture.

Stabiae

The ancient city of Stabiae was destroyed by the Roman general Sulla when he conquered Pompeii and made it a Roman colony. But many beautiful villas were built in the area. Pictures cut from the walls of these villas during the haphazard excavating of the eighteenth century can be seen in the small Museum at Stabiae, while others grace the Museo Nazionale at Naples. The largest villa uncovered in the recent excavations has a huge swimming pool surrounded by a colonnade. From the villa the owners enjoyed a magnificent view of the Bay and Vesuvius beyond. Little did the inhabitants of these beautiful villas suspect that Vesuvius which rose in calm and stark majesty would one day suddenly awake and destroy them all. It was to Pomponianus living in a villa at Stabiae that Pliny the Elder hastened to give help. He and his friends hoped to make an escape by sea, but this was impossible; the waters of the Bay were wild and running in a contrary direction. Pliny lay down on a discarded sail on the shore and called for cold water. But overcome by the gases from Vesuvius he died.

For the visitor who tarries at Pompeii the ancient city lives again. The old *custode* dozing in the summer sun rouses himself as we approach. Though long ago officially retired, he returns faithfully each day to his post. Tourists seldom venture to the unfrequented spot where he keeps his vigil. With unself-conscious dignity he bids us "sit and rest" ourselves, and offers a paper bag filled with fruit gathered from his orchard as he inquires about the progress of our work in the excavations. We discuss the probable yield of the vineyard in the garden of a house nearby, in which we have been working. It is "sufficient only for the needs of the family," we decide, for the vineyard is similar in size to the one owned by the old *custode,* which provides him with his "quart a day." The modern Pompeian still makes the wine from his own vines, just as his ancient forebears did; each autumn the ripened grapes are still trod with bare feet. Life continues much as it always has in the shadow of Vesuvius.

Often on leaving the excavations, we have stopped to admire the flower garden belonging to another *custode,* who lives just outside the ancient city wall. In the garden is a household shrine similar to those we have seen in the excavated city. But our friend places a bouquet of flowers in front of his shrine, instead of decorating it with a garland. And inside is a little statue of the Virgin of Pompeii, instead of Venus Pompeiana. On one occasion we found three shrines in the garden of an ancient house. As we studied them a workman commented, "The people who lived in this house were *molto religiosi.*" He went on to add, "I have only one lavarium in my house."

Generations of workmen have bequeathed to their sons skills perfected in disinterring the buried city. The many *custodi* who guard the excavated city speak knowingly of the houses and their ancient occupants. In the evening as we return to our *albergo* we are sometimes greeted by a young custodian reporting for night duty; in former years his aged father always greeted us in the evening as we went out by the amphitheater gate.

On arriving at our hotel one night we found it decked in gala attire with garlands made of shining leaves. We exclaimed with delight for they were exactly the same as the garlands painted on the walls of an ancient house that we had been photographing that very day! (A few days later we were to find the same type of luxurious garlands decorating the ancient theater, for the production of the *Birds* of Aristophanes – a play that may well have been given in ancient Pompeii.) The *Albergo del Rosario* was making ready for the *Nozze d'Argento e d'Oro,* a great celebration to be held the next day, for which people would come from throughout Italy to repeat again, on their silver or golden anniversary, their marriage vows in the Sanctuary of Pompeii, dedicated to the Virgin of the Rosary. The next morning a red carpet reached from the *Albergo* to the *Santuario.* As we watched, the procession began, led by a dignified couple in the colorful costume of Sardinia who had come to celebrate their golden wedding. Pompeii has always had its riligious processions. Today it is the Sanctuary that draws thousands of pilgrims to the modern city. But the greatest festa is in the month of May; the streets are thronged as thousands parade in honor of the Madonna of the Rosary. Today it is the Madonna of Pompeii and not Venus Pompeiana that is honored.

Located near the Sanctuary are various charitable institutions, including orphanages which are a refuge for children from all Italy. One afternoon as we visited with the Sister who had in her charge the littlest orphans, a very small one, chubby and curly-haired, shyly reached out hands to us in an invitation to be lifted up. We were reminded of little Successus, whose portrait was found by the excavators where it had been painted on the wall of his father's home after the child had died.

The Pompeians have not changed. The small shops that line the streets of modern Pompeii are similar in size to those in the excavated city. The friendly grocer sitting in front of his shop reminds us of another ancient portrait . . . We remember our visit with a great Pompeian scholar. As we sat in his garden and read the inscription painted by admiring friends on his wall, he evoked for us the inhabitants of the ancient city, and as he talked with understanding, he became as one of them. Little wonder that he has been called the "most Pompeian of them all."

Land, water, mountains, – even the people are the same. Venus, ancient Italian goddess of gardens, still watches over the fertile Campanian countryside and Flora brings forth her flowers as of old.

THE PLATES

Cover: The Forum at Pompeii

The Forum was the civic, religious, and business center about which were grouped most of the important buildings of the city.

View of Pompeii from a Tower of the City Wall

From the Tower of Mercury on the northern city wall, the visitor has an impressive panoramic view of the ancient city of Pompeii, situated in the fertile plain of Campania. Beyond the plain rise the Lattari Mountains. Turning to the right, (not in the picture) the visitor can see the mountains finally sink into the Bay at the promontory of Sorrento and rise again as the isle of Capri. To the left, cornfields grow on top of the unexcavated portions of the city. Behind is Mt. Vesuvius. The incomparable beauty of the area – mountains, fertile plain and Bay – can all be seen in one sweeping glance. Then the eye lingers to pick out details. Individual houses can be identified, some with roofs carefully restored, and with trees and flowers growing again in the enclosed gardens.

had been built. From the terraces of these homes, owners could enjoy the spectacular panorama of the plain below, and the mountains and the Bay beyond.

View of Misenum from Lake Avernus

From Misenum Pliny the Younger, as a boy of seventeen, witnessed the eruption of Vesuvius in A. D. 79, which he later described in two famous letters to the Roman historian Tacitus. The dark and gloomy waters of Lake Avernus led the Romans to believe that it was the site of the entrance to the underworld.

Venus Marina

This impressive painting of Venus floating in from the sea on a sea-shell accompanied by two Cupids was found on the back garden wall of a beautiful house excavated in 1952. Venus was one of the most important deities at Pompeii. A very different representation of Venus is found on the famous shop sign of the cloth-maker M. Vecilius Verecundus, which shows a dignified and fully clothed Venus Pompeiana.

Volcanic Ledge on which Pompeii was Built

The site of ancient Pompeii was both created and destroyed by Vesuvius for the city was built on a huge stream of lava which had flowed down the sides of Vesuvius in prehistoric times. On the southwest edge of the city the lava flow had stopped abruptly, giving the city an easily fortified boundary. Here the wall had been removed, perhaps as early as the second century B. C. and luxurious homes

Sacrifice Scene on Altar

On the front of the marble altar which still stands in the courtyard of the Temple of Vespasian, is depicted the sacrifice scene which took place when the temple was dedicated. The *victimarius* leads forth the bull, which he is about to slay, while the priest, with covered head, pours a libation, preparatory to conducting the sacrifice. Standing nearby are a flute-player, two lictors with their bundles of rods, and boys with the utensils to be used during the sacrifice.

Electoral Notice

Electoral notices cover the facades of houses and shops in Pompeii. On the outside of his restaurant Masculus had painted a notice in which he urged people to "make Cn. Helvius aedile, because he is worthy of public office": CN. HELVIVM SABINVM AED(ILEM) D(IGNVM) R(E) P(VBLICA) O(RO) V(OS) F(ACIATIS). The two aediles were the magistrates whose duties included keeping the city streets clean, supervising the city market, the public baths, and putting on the public games.

Stepping Stones at Street Intersection

Deep ruts were worn in the lava paving stones by the heavy wheeled-traffic that passed up and down the Via Stabia, the most important traffic artery of Pompeii. Goods carried from the port to the suburbs and villas to the north traveled on this street. The axles of the wagons and carts were high enough to clear the stepping stones which were necessary for pedestrians during heavy rains.

Mercury

Mercury, god of merchants, was a popular deity in the commercial city of Pompeii; he is frequently shown carrying a money bag. One of the sons of the family may have posed for this portrait of the god, found in the house of Marcus Lucretius Fronto. It is a more charming representation than most.

House of the Faun

Time and the bombs of World War II have taken their toll, but this palatial house, with its two atriums, two handsome peristyle gardens, and four dining-rooms (for spring, summer, autumn, and winter), is still stately in its elegance.

Bacchus, God of Wine

This interesting painting (now in the Museo Nazionale in Naples), found on a household shrine in Pompeii, shows Bacchus, god of wine, crowned with grape leaves and clothed with huge clusters of grapes. Vineyards grow on the lower slopes of a mountain – probably Vesuvius before the eruption of A. D. 79. The many house shrines found in Pompeii not only give information about family worship but they often throw light on the family itself. The two snakes frequently painted on these shrines were probably symbols of the Genius of the master and of the mistress of the house; the male snake can be recognized by its big crest. The single crested snake on this shrine suggests that a bachelor lived in the palatial house in which it was found. The house is believed to be the residence of Titus Claudius Verus whose little sweetheart had put up an election notice asking people to vote for him. The luxuriousness of the house indicates that the owner was a young man of considerable wealth. The painting suggests that his wealth might have come in part, at least, from vineyards on Mt. Vesuvius.

Wine-Press in the Villa of the Mysteries

Pompeii was an important wine-center, and much of the wine sold in the city was produced in nearby villas. The restored wine-press in the Villa of the Mysteries near Pompeii indicates that wine was an important source of income for the owner.

Worshipers of Bacchus

The room adjacent to the nuptial chamber in the Villa of the Mysteries is decorated with scenes depicting the initiation of the mistress of the villa into the Mysteries of Bacchus. The initiate is given a ritual flogging, and after the initiation dances in ecstasy.

Garden Painting in the House of Venus Marina

Owners frequently made their gardens appear much larger by painting a picture of a garden on the wall enclosing it. Fountains, trees and statues too large to be contained in the actual garden could be included in the painted one. In this painting, behind a low lattice fence, the ever-present oleander, roses, myrtle, laurel, ivy, and other plants grow in profusion. Birds fly through the air, two rest on the rim of the splashing fountain; two gray herons walk along the fence. The small painted niche is a shrine which once held the small statues of the household gods.

The Garden of M. Loreius Tiburtinus

One of the most beautiful gardens at Pompeii was found in the home of

Loreius Tiburtinus, a worshiper of the Egyptian goddess, Isis. A miniature "Nile" River, which was perhaps flooded on religious holidays, flowed the length of the vine-covered terrace at the back of the house, and continued down the length of the garden laid out on a lower level. This beautiful enclosed garden comprised most of a city block, and was graced with arbored walks, an orchard of fine fruit trees, flowering shrubs, fountains, and statues.

Fountain Statue

This charming putto held a sea-shell from which water jetted into the basin below.

Street Scene in Ancient Pompeii

The homes on this street show the patchwork construction that resulted when miscellaneous materials from buildings destroyed by the earthquake were used in rebuilding the city.

Vesuvius from the Amphitheater

The amphitheater at Pompeii is the oldest known Roman amphitheater. Built by the Romans shortly after Pompeii was made a Roman colony, it had a seating capacity of about 20,000. This was large enough to seat the entire population, with room left for the visitors from neighboring towns, who thronged the city when entertainments were held. Huge signs painted on the walls at Pompeii and even on tombs attest the great popularity of the shows in the amphitheater. The gladiators were the chief features, but wild animal hunts, prize fighters, and wrestlers were also popular.

Prize fighter

This mosaic floor is now in the Museo Nazionale in Naples.

Modern Pompeii from the Amphitheater

The dome of the Sanctuary of the *Madonna del Rosario* and the adjacent campanile dominate the skyline of modern Pompeii. Various charitable institutions are clustered about the Sanctuary, which was begun in 1876, and consecrated in 1891. A humble, miraculous painting representing the Virgin and Child with St. Dominic and St. Catharine, found in a rubbish cart in 1875, has ever since been attracting thousands and thousands of pilgrims every year from all parts of the world, and has made the Sanctuary a world famous healing shrine and the goal of many pilgrimages.

View toward the Lattari Mountains from the Palaestra

The great Palaestra, located across from the Amphitheater, was larger than the Forum. Here the Pompeian youths excercised and held their competitions. The huge swimming pool in the center was bordered by a double row of plane trees that furnished shade for the athletes. The wide porticoes which surrounded three sides of the Palaestra housed visiting athletes and furnished shelter for the crowds when sudden storms gathered during a show in the amphitheater.

Aristocratic Houses at Herculaneum

The beautiful homes in the southern part of the city had garden terraces from which there was a spectacular panoramic view over the Bay of Naples.

Excavating Ancient Herculaneum from under Modern Resina

Excavation progresses slowly; the rocklike fill which encases the city is extremely difficult to remove.

Fertile Campania

Modern gardens just outside the walls of ancient Pompeii are laid out in rectangular plots separated by paths which are used also as irrigation channels, exactly as in ancient gardens.

Dam on the Sarno River

The Sarno, today, furnishes water for irrigating the gardens of Pompeii. The rich Campanian soil still produces the cabbages and onions for which Pompeii was famous in antiquity, but irrigation is still necessary and water is expensive. Early in the morning the vegetable man can be seen selling his produce; his patient donkey stops at each entrance, while the peddler supplies his customers and fills the housewives' baskets let down from balconies.

"Flora"

This charming little picture of a lithesome girl gathering flowers in a meadow, is one of the finest works produced by Campanian painters. It bears the title of "Flora" or "Primavera" in the Museo Nazionale. It is one of four tiny pictures found in a villa at Stabiae, when excavations were begun there in the eighteenth century.

The Shore at Stabiae

Today the buildings of Castellammare di Stabia rise along the shore where Pliny the Elder lost his life while trying to rescue friends during the eruption of Vesuvius in A. D. 79.

The authors wish to express their appreciation to Professore Alfonso de Franciscis, Il Soprintendente alle Antichità della Campania, whose gracious cooperation did so much to facilitate their work in the ancient cities of Campania.

PANORAMA-BOOKS

USA: ARIZONA* · CALIFORNIA · FLORIDA · LOS ANGELES* · NEW YORK
SAN FRANCISCO · WASHINGTON, D.C.

Germany: BAVARIA · BAVARIAN ROYAL CASTLES · BERLIN · THE BLACK
FOREST · BONN · COLOGNE · ESSEN · HAMBURG · HEIDELBERG · LAKE
CONSTANCE · MOSELLE · MUNICH · THE RHINE · ROMANTIC GERMANY
THE RUHR

Austria: AUSTRIA · BADGASTEIN · CARINTHIA · SALZBURG AND SUR-
ROUNDINGS · STYRIA · TYROL · VIENNA

France: ALSACE · BRITTANY · CHÂTEAUX OF THE LOIRE · CORSICA
CÔTE D'AZUR · FRENCH CATHEDRALS · MONT SAINT-MICHEL · NOR-
MANDY · PARIS · PARIS BY NIGHT · PROVENCE

Italy: CAPRI · FLORENCE · THE GULF OF NAPLES · POMPEII · ROME
SICILY · SOUTH TYROL · VENICE

Scandinavia: COPENHAGEN · FINLAND · LAND OF THE MIDNIGHT SUN
NORWAY · SWEDEN

Switzerland: GRISONS · LAKE GENEVA · SWITZERLAND · ROMANTIC
SWITZERLAND

Capitals of the world: BRUSSELS · ISTANBUL · LONDON · MOSCOW · PEKING
RIO DE JANEIRO

Other countries: ANDALUSIA · BALEARIC ISLANDS · BERMUDA · CANADA
FLANDERS · GREECE · THE HOLY LAND · ICELAND · IRELAND · ISRAEL
JAMAICA · JAPAN · MEXICO · MOROCCO* · NASSAU · THE NETHER-
LANDS · PORTUGAL · PUERTO RICO* · SCOTLAND · SPAIN · VIRGIN
ISLANDS* · YUGOSLAVIA – Dalmatian Coast

* *In preparation*   EDITOR HANS ANDERMANN

£1500_